The Pebble® First Guide to

Wildcats

by Zachary Pitts

Consulting Editor: Gail Saunders-Smith, PhD

Consultant: Tanya Dewey, PhD
University of Michigan Museum of Zoology

Capstone
press®

Mankato, Minnesota

Pebble Books are published by Capstone Press,
151 Good Counsel Drive, P.O. Box 669, Mankato, Minnesota 56002.
www.capstonepress.com

1 2 3 4 5 6 13 12 11 10 09 08

Library of Congress Cataloging-in-Publication Data
Pitts, Zachary.
    The Pebble first guide to wildcats / by Zachary Pitts.
    p. cm. — (Pebble books. Pebble first guides)
    Includes bibliographical references and index.
    ISBN-13: 978-1-4296-1709-3 (hardcover)
    ISBN-10: 1-4296-1709-8 (hardcover)
    ISBN-13: 978-1-4296-2803-7 (softcover pbk.)
    ISBN-10: 1-4296-2803-0 (softcover pbk.)
    1. Wildcat — Juvenile literature. I. Title. II. Series.
QL737.C23P558 2009
599.75 — dc22   2008001400

Summary: A basic field guide format introduces 13 wildcat species. Includes color
    photographs and range maps.

About Wildcat Lengths

The lengths given in this book for each wildcat species
measure the cat from head to tail.

Note to Parents and Teachers

The Pebble First Guides set supports science standards related
to life science. In a reference format, this book describes and
illustrates 13 wildcat species. This book introduces early readers
to subject-specific vocabulary words, which are defined in the
Glossary section. Early readers may need assistance to read some
words and to use the Table of Contents, Glossary, Read More,
Internet Sites, and Index sections of the book.

Table of Contents

Bobcat

Length:	2 to 4 feet (.6 to 1.2 meters)
Weight:	20 to 26 pounds (9 to 12 kilograms)
Eats:	rabbits, rodents, birds
Lives:	forests, swamps
Facts:	• very short tail
	• lives 12 to 13 years

Bobcat Range

☐ southern Canada to northern Mexico

cubs

Canada Lynx

Length:	2 to 3 feet (.6 to 1 meter)
Weight:	10 to 37 pounds (4.5 to 17 kilograms)
Eats:	snowshoe hares, rodents
Lives:	forests
Facts:	• long, pointed fur on ears
	• big paws help it walk on snow

Canada Lynx Range

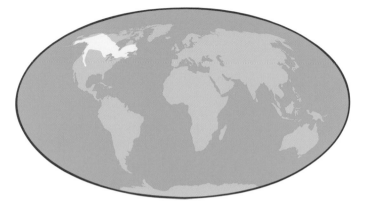

☐ Canada, northern United States

cub

Caracal

Say It: KAR-uh-kal

Length: 3.5 to 5 feet (1 to 1.5 meters)

Weight: 22 to 40 pounds (10 to 18 kilograms)

Eats: birds, rabbits, rodents

Lives: dry plains

Facts:
- also called a desert lynx
- long black hair on ear tips

Caracal Range

☐ Africa, southwest Asia

cub

Cheetah

Length: 6 to 7.5 feet (2 to 2.3 meters)

Weight: 80 to 140 pounds (36 to 64 kilograms)

Eats: gazelles, antelope, birds

Lives: dry plains

Facts:
- fastest land animal
- hunts during the day

Cheetah Range

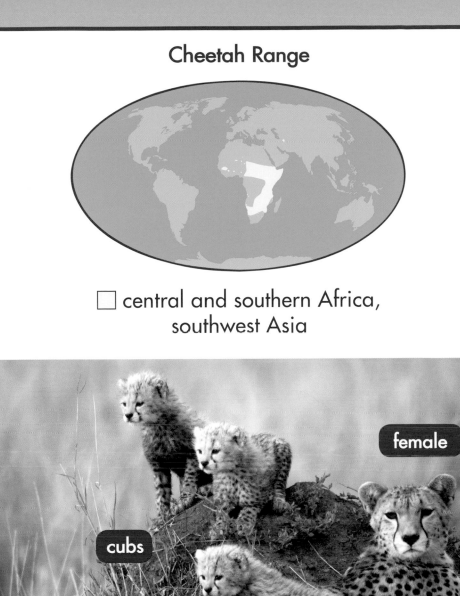

☐ central and southern Africa,
southwest Asia

female

cubs

Clouded Leopard

Length: 4 to 5.5 feet (1.2 to 1.7 meters)

Weight: 24 to 44 pounds (11 to 20 kilograms)

Eats: deer, monkeys, birds

Lives: rain forests

Facts:
- also called a mint leopard
- hunts from trees

Clouded Leopard Range

☐ southeast Asia

cub

Length:	5 to 10 feet (1.5 to 3 meters)
Weight:	79 to 348 pounds (36 to 158 kilograms)
Eats:	peccaries, large rodents
Lives:	forests, swamps
Facts:	• largest cat in Central and South America
	• some have black fur

Jaguar Range

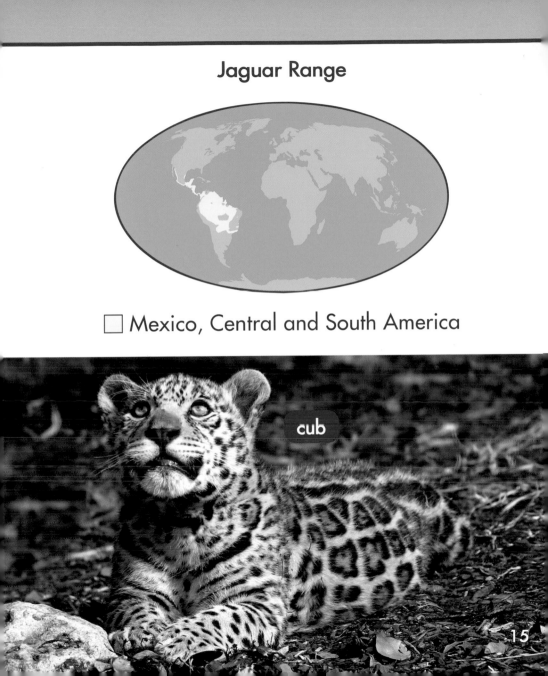

☐ Mexico, Central and South America

cub

Leopard

Length:	5 to 11 feet (1.5 to 3.4 meters)
Weight:	57 to 200 pounds (26 to 91 kilograms)
Eats:	antelope, gazelles, monkeys
Lives:	forests, mountains, plains
Facts:	• good climber
	• carries prey up trees

Leopard Range

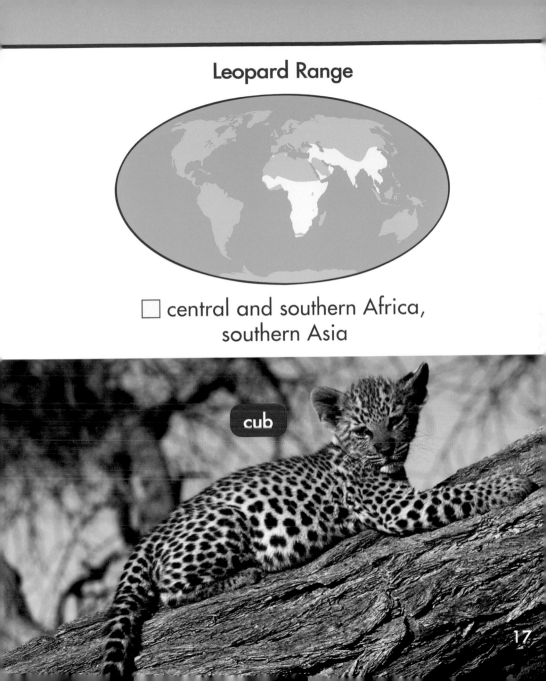

☐ central and southern Africa, southern Asia

cub

Lion

female

male

Length:	6.5 to 11.5 feet (2 to 3.5 meters)
Weight:	227 to 600 pounds (103 to 272 kilograms)
Eats:	zebras, buffalo, antelope, wildebeest
Lives:	grassy plains
Facts:	• roar can be heard from miles away
	• only wildcat that lives in groups

Lion Range

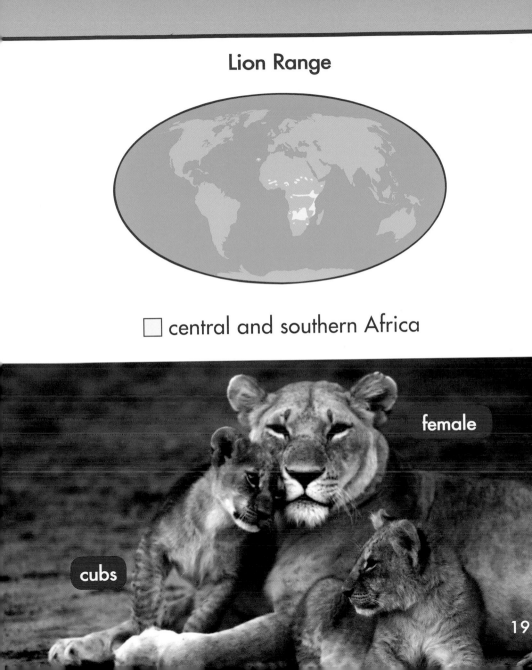

☐ central and southern Africa

female

cubs

Length: 3 to 4.5 feet (.9 to 1.4 meters)

Weight: 20 to 25 pounds (9 to 11.5 kilograms)

Eats: rodents, reptiles, birds

Lives: rain forests

Facts:
- twice the size of a pet cat
- good swimmer and climber

Ocelot Range

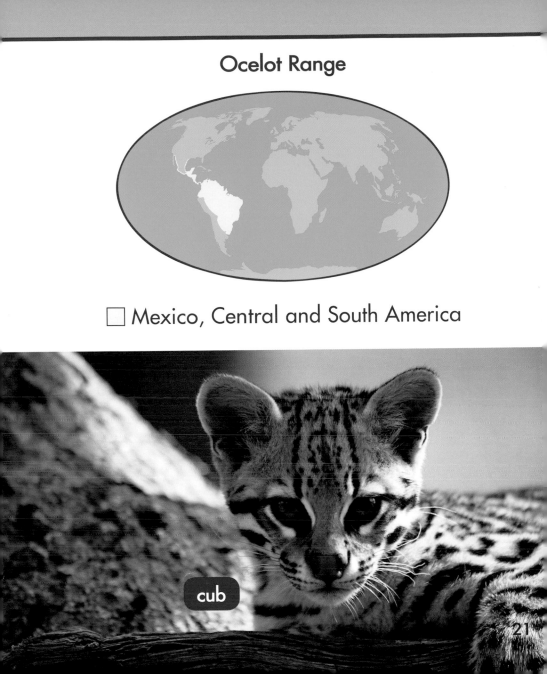

☐ Mexico, Central and South America

cub

Puma

Length:	5 to 10.5 feet (1.5 to 3.25 meters)
Weight:	75 to 264 pounds (34 to 120 kilograms)
Eats:	deer, rabbits, large rodents
Lives:	forests, mountains, swamps, plains
Facts:	• also called a cougar, mountain lion, or panther
	• can jump 16 feet (5 meters) high

Puma Range

☐ western and southern North America, Central and South America

cubs

Serval

Length:	3 to 4.5 feet (.9 to 1.4 meters)
Weight:	20 to 40 pounds (9 to 18 kilograms)
Eats:	rodents, birds, reptiles
Lives:	wet plains
Facts:	• hears better than any wildcat
	• leaps high into air to grab birds

24

Serval Range

☐ Africa

cub

Snow Leopard

Length:	6 to 7.5 feet (2 to 2.3 meters)
Weight:	75 to 165 pounds (35 to 75 kilograms)
Eats:	sheep, goats, large rodents
Lives:	snowy mountains
Facts:	• big paws help it walk on snow
	• tail used to balance while jumping
	• endangered

Snow Leopard Range

☐ central Asia

cubs

Tiger

Length:	7 to 11 feet (2 to 3.4 meters)
Weight:	165 to 675 pounds (75 to 306 kilograms)
Eats:	deer, wild pigs
Lives:	forests, swamps
Facts:	• world's largest cat
	• spends time in water
	• endangered

Tiger Range

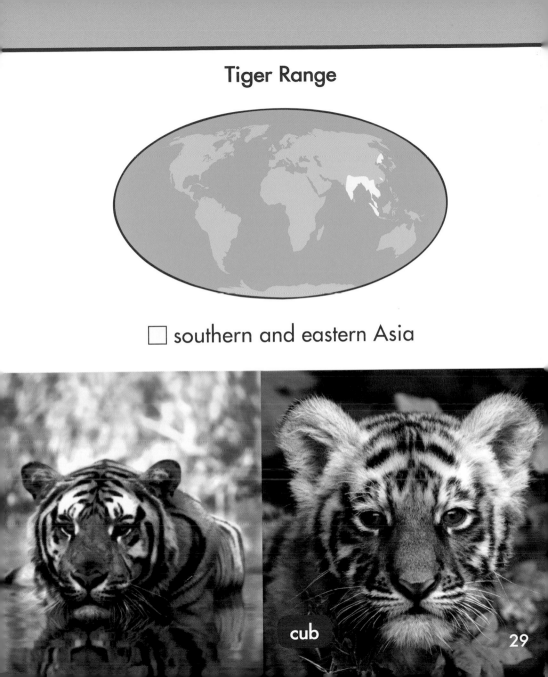

☐ southern and eastern Asia

cub

Glossary

antelope — an animal that looks like a large deer and runs very fast

endangered — at risk of dying out

gazelle — a small antelope found in Africa and Asia; gazelles run very fast.

hare — an animal that looks like a large rabbit with long, strong back legs

peccary — an animal that is related to a pig

plain — a large, flat area of land with few trees

prey — an animal hunted by another animal for food

reptile — a cold-blooded animal with a backbone; scales cover a reptile's body.

rodent — a mammal with long front teeth used for gnawing

Read More

Landau, Elaine. *Big Cats: Hunters of the Night.* Animals after Dark. Berkeley Heights, N.J.: Enslow Elementary, 2008.

Shea, Therese. *Wild Cats.* Big Bad Biters. New York: PowerKids Press, 2007.

Internet Sites

FactHound offers a safe, fun way to find Internet sites related to this book. All of the sites on FactHound have been researched by our staff.

Here's how:

1. Visit *www.facthound.com*
2. Choose your grade level.
3. Type in this book ID **1429617098** for age-appropriate sites. You may also browse subjects by clicking on letters, or by clicking on pictures and words.
4. Click on the **Fetch It** button.

FactHound will fetch the best sites for you!

Index

Grade: 1
Early-Intervention Level: 24

Editorial Credits

Erika L. Shores, editor; Alison Thiele, designer; Danielle Ceminsky, map illustrator; Jo Miller, photo researcher

Photo Credits

Alamy/blinkwinkel/Lohmann, 25; Linda Kennedy, 21; Papilio/Robert Pickett, 7
Bruce Coleman Inc., 13; D. Robert Franz, 26; Frank Parker, 11; Lynn M. Stone, 12; Mark Newman, 8; Tom Brakefield, 27
Corel, 29 (left)
iStockphoto/Davina Graham, cover (cougar); Roman Kobzarev, cover (cheetah); Stuart Berman, cover (tiger)
Nature Picture Library/Ingo Arndt, 9
Peter Arnold/BIOS Bios - Auteurs Klien J. -L. & Hubert M. -L., 5; BIOS Klien & Hubert, 14; Biosphoto/BIOS Auters (droits geres) Boulton Mark, 19; Bruce Lichtenberger, 6; Martin Harvey, 17, 24; P. Oxford, 20
Shutterstock/Bruce J. Lichtenberger, 23; EcoPrint, 18 (left); Ferenc Cegledi, 28; FloridaStock, 22; Jeff Carpenter, cover (lion); Keith Levit, 18 (right); Larsek, 10; Robynrg, 4; Ronnie Howard, 15; Snowleopard1, 29 (right); Stuart Taylor, 16